Credit Power

Taking Control of your Credit, Life &

Freedom

Saloam Knox

ISBN: 978-0-578-82879-4

Book design by Hoveify
LRC Editing
Academy of Visions Publishing

Printed by Amazon KDP, Inc., in the United States of America.
First printing edition 2021.

Creditpowerllc.com

Dedication Page

I would like to dedicate this book to my daughter Paris, who has been with me on this journey. She has witnessed my evolution and the changes that I am still making daily.

To my daughter (Pretty Faces),

Mommy wants you to know that everything you need is already inside of you. You are a;
P*recious*
A*mazing*
R*esilient*
I*ntelligent*
S*oul*

I love you.

Table of Contents

Introduction

"For I know the plans I have for you declares the Lord, Plans to prosper you, and not to harm you, plans to give you hope and a future." – Jeremiah 29:11

I walked into the job interview with my best professional attire, a bright smile, and a positive attitude. I was confident and prepared for all the questions that would come my way. Finally, I was given an opportunity that would help change my life for the better. I was tired of working temporary jobs for a few weeks at a time and barely making ends meet. I was over the government assistance and living in section 8 housing. I wanted better for my child and myself, and I knew that if I wanted more for us, I would have to make some adjustments to improve my financial status. I knew if I could land the job at the credit union, I could really take control of my life. As I walked into the office for my interview, I was excited but also a bit nervous. I shook his hand, took my seat, and took a deep breath. He began asking me questions. I was able to answer each question without any hesitation. The more we talked, the better I felt. The interview was going great; I felt comfortable and confident. As the interview progressed, he shared that he was a veteran, and I felt an instant connection because I, too, am a veteran. We opened up and shared our experience with going to war and serving our country, having both served in 9/11: Operation Enduring Freedom. Everything felt right, and I couldn't have asked for the interview to go any better. We shook hands and he assured me that he would be in contact. I left feeling great and extremely optimistic about my future with the credit union. I thought to myself, "This is it, Saloam. It's time to change your life."

A couple of days passed, and I hadn't heard anything. I expected to hear back from them much sooner. Although I thought it was odd that things were moving so slowly, I was still optimistic. After all, the interview was a success, so there was no reason for me to be worried. I had only prepared myself for a successful outcome giving how smoothly the interview went. With each passing day, I became a little less confident and I grew a little more concerned. I finally received correspondence concerning the job. To my dismay, I was told that I hadn't been selected for the position. I was utterly devastated and extremely confused. The interview had gone perfectly. I looked great, I had a positive attitude, and I answered every question precisely. I even connected with the interviewer, and we shared war stories. I wondered to myself what could have possibly gone wrong. I just knew I was the perfect candidate for the job and couldn't understand why I didn't get it. My disappointment evolved into depression, and my optimism turned into defeat. I felt like my world was crumbling. There I was, with no job, no money, and no hope. I didn't know what I was going to do. As the days went by, I could not seem to pull myself out of the slumps. My future was riding on this opportunity. I racked my brain, trying to make sense of it all. After replaying the interview over and over in my head, I decided to go back to the credit union and find out exactly why I didn't get the job. I was convinced that surely there had to have been a mistake in the selection process.

When I arrived at the credit union, I requested to speak to the gentleman that interviewed me. When I got into his office, I wasted no time. I asked why I hadn't been hired for the position. He looked over some documents, and then he looked up at me and said, "Ms. Saloam, your interview went great." I was perplexed by his response; I'm sure the look of confusion on my face let him know that I didn't understand. There was a long pause as he continued reviewing the documents in his hand. He looked up at me and said, “However, when we ran a credit check, there were some items on your credit report that were alarming. Based on the information obtained, you wouldn’t be a good fit for this position.” I didn’t understand, because my credit score was in the 700s. How could I not be a good candidate? I left the office even more confused than I was when I first arrived. I began wondering what my credit report said about me. I didn’t get the job because my character on paper told a completely different story than what I portrayed in the interview. I still did not fully understand how my credit prevented me from getting a job, though. I thought that having a good score was all I needed. I wondered what exactly they were looking for.

I requested a copy of my credit report. I needed to see what prevented me from landing the job with the credit union. I found out that from 2003-2012, I was being taken advantage of by some of my family members. I was devastated when I learned that the people that I trusted the most were scamming me. Unfortunately, I had to face the harsh reality that I was the victim of identity theft. After reviewing my credit report, I learned that there were tickets, hospital bills, phone bills, cable bills, and even bounced checks attached to my name. My family members were using my identity. I felt completely overwhelmed by my reality and my world seemed to be spiraling out of control. Not only did I not get the job, but I was left to restore my credit and I didn't know where to begin. The thought of cleaning my credit up felt completely overwhelming.

I honestly just wanted to give up. I did not have anything, and at the rate my life was going, it felt like it would always be that way. I came so close to throwing in the towel, but there was something inside of me that believed I could have a better life. I am reminded of the scripture, *"Trust in the Lord with all your heart and lean not to your own understanding" –Proverbs 3:5.* Even though I did not get my dream job, or even though my loved ones turned their back on me, I didn't give up. I still knew that there was something inside of me that was greater than my circumstances. I decided to pick myself up off the ground and build again. I had to start by fixing my credit so that I could fix my life.

There is a famous quote that says, "You're not responsible for how you are raised, but you're fully responsible for how you turn out." I had to take that same approach with my credit. Although I wasn't responsible for the identity theft, it was my complete responsibility to straighten it out. My credit report told a story about me that did not line up with what I was saying. In the interview, I said I was trustworthy, but my credit report said I didn't pay back money. In the interview, I said I was dependable, but my credit report showed delinquencies. He listened to my story during the interview, but my credit report did not validate my story.

I was uncomfortable with my credit report telling a

story about me that I was ashamed of. I wanted my credit report to validate that I am trustworthy and dependable. Therefore, I buckled down and got serious about fixing my credit. I had to decide if I wanted to be the victim or the victor. I could no longer hold on to what was done to me, so I made the decision to let it go. Holding on to what was done to me wasn't helping me to change my circumstances and was keeping me stuck. The bible speaks about forgiving and letting things go, "*And forgive us our debts, as we also have forgiven our debtors*" – *Matthew 6:12.*

I began working to repair my credit, I took my score from a 400 to an 849. I held myself accountable. I could not go back and change the past, but I had full control over my present and my future. I got serious about it, and my credit score started going up. I was no longer in a place of despair; things were looking up for me. I was so excited; I wanted to share with everyone that it's possible for them to fix their credit as well. I recruited friends and family members, and they started to make changes to fix their credit, also. I became more invested in learning about credit, and I started helping others. I realized that repairing credit was the answer that so many people needed. I discovered that if I educate our communities on financial literacy, I could be a catalyst for creating a better future.

In 2014, I launched *Credit Power, LLC*, and I help empower our people to adopt financial abundance regardless of their socioeconomic status. I help give people a second chance at life and help them move towards financial freedom and increase generational wealth. I don't want people to allow their circumstances to define their future. We all have the power to change our narrative. I am devoted to educating everyone that I can on financial literacy. For those of you who are on the brink of giving up because things don't seem to be getting better financially, this book is a tool to help you repair your credit so you can improve your life.

CREDIT POWER SUSTAINABILITY CHART

The chart below was created by Credit Power, LLC. This chart provides a breakdown of the characteristics and traits that are considered when viewing your credit report. When compared to your Fico pie chart you will see how each section explained coincides with the five components of your credit. Each section will be explained in full detail throughout this book.

Present condition	Foundation	Stability	Management Skills	Trustworthiness
Risky, in a crisis, In trouble Possible bankruptcy 6 or more Inquiries	Able to multitask Flexible Revolving Installment Versatile Mixture	Length of experience Reliability Longer history Predicts % risk of borrower not repaying their loans	Credit experience Spending habits Living above means Patience Delayed gratification, Responsible	Liar or Thief? Say what you mean and mean what you say. Good payment history Lack of knowledge
10%	10%	15%	30%	35%

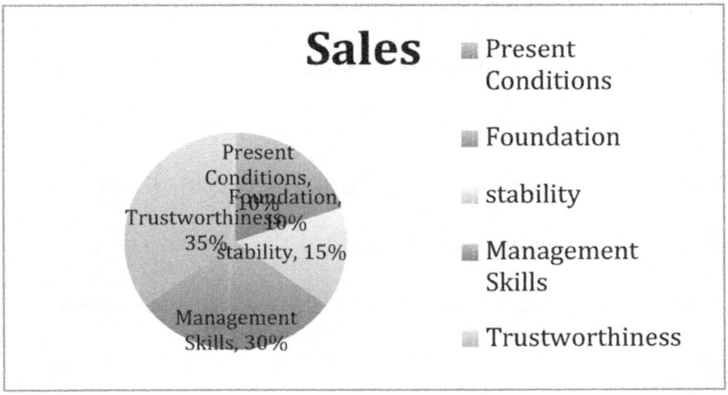

1

Present Conditions

When I didn't get the job of my dreams in 2012, I was devastated. I came so close to walking away from everyone and everything. Avoiding my circumstances felt easier than actually dealing with them at the time. However, I am here to tell you that avoiding the problem will not solve the problem. The longer you take to address the issue, the bigger the problem will become. I was exhausted by the thought of just taking the initial steps towards creating better for myself. If you want the best out of life you must do the work. Even the bible provides reference regarding putting in work, *"A sluggard's appetite is never filled, but the desires of the diligent are fully satisfied" – Proverbs 13:4*. I knew that I did not want to continue struggling through life, so I had to evaluate my life conditions. I began asking myself what my present conditions said about me. When I sat back and really evaluated the answer, I was not happy with what I saw. The way I was living my life was detrimental to my future and I had to figure out what needed to be done to evoke positive change. When I took a closer look, I began to understand that I wasn't stable. I was jumping around from job to job. My living conditions were not the best, and those around me weren't doing well either. Your environment can be the catalyst of growth or it can be a bed of destruction. My environment was definitely a bed of destruction for my future. I wanted better for myself, but I didn't put myself in the position to receive better. It is so easy to lie around wishing for better, without ever taking the necessary actions towards becoming better. I had to change my behavior. It was no longer enough for me to just sit around wishing for things to be different. I had to make a declaration to myself that I would begin taking the necessary action steps towards creating the life I wanted to live. However, there were setbacks and disappointments that made it very difficult at times. There were moments when I lost faith and optimism, but I always found a way to push myself. I decided not to sit back and allow life to just happen to me and began seeing my circumstances from a different perspective. Instead of viewing my circumstances as disappointments, I started viewing them as opportunities. I viewed rejection as opportunity for an even better *yes.* I became motivated to fix my life. Yes, I still had to overcome emotional hurdles, but I kept going. I was often reminded of the feelings of shame, embarrassment, and defeat. However, I used those negative feelings as fuel to keep going. Every time I thought about my credit keeping me from getting the job that I so desperately wanted, it pushed me harder. I used every negative emotion to push me towards better when I was at my lowest. I'm reminded of the scripture, *"I press toward the mark for the prize of the high calling of God in Christ Jesus" – Philippians 3:14.*

Yes, there were days when I wanted to stay in bed. Yes, there were moments when I felt sorry for myself. However, I realized that I had to do the work so that I could change the outcome. Nothing works, without work! *"Let us not become weary in doing good, for at the proper time we will reap a harvest if we do not give up" –Galatians 6:9.*

I began to understand that it was entirely up to me to re-write my story, and I could not give anyone else the power to write the narrative for me. Not being hired at the credit union was only one part of my journey. My story didn't stop there, and neither did I. When we prematurely give up on ourselves, we relinquish our power to change our narrative.

The first step towards changing my outcome was educating myself about credit. The more knowledge we have, the further we can go. Starting out, I didn't know much about credit at all. I only knew that I needed to maintain a high score. I had no idea that there were many other components that contributed to my score and my overall report. In the beginning, I had so many questions, but I started with understanding what credit is.

Credit is receiving something now with a commitment to pay for it later. I'll break it down a little more using a very simple example. Have you ever left home without money? Once you realized you didn't have the money, you may have asked your friend or family member to spot you until later. Once they paid for your bill, you instantly owed them. That was a credit exchange. You were able to get something immediately with the ability to pay for it later. While the overall process of credit includes more steps, you now understand the concept of how credit works. So now you may be wondering, how does credit work? When dealing with financial institutions that know nothing about you, they rely on your credit report and your credit score to help them to determine if they should approve or deny you. Your credit worthiness is determined by the information provided in your credit report.

Credit Score

Your credit report offers information regarding your credit history. Let's break down the different ranges of credit scores. An excellent credit score is between 800-850. There are great perks that come along with having an excellent credit score. You can expect very low-interest rates along with the best terms and conditions. Essentially, the higher your score, the better treatment you will receive from lenders and you are more likely to be approved for the things you desire. Those who have credit scores between 750-799 are in great shape and will receive similar treatment as those who have a credit score in the 800s. 700-749 is still considered good credit, and those who fall into this range will qualify for most loans. However, interest rates will be slightly higher than those who have a 750 and above. 650-699 is considered fair credit. Interest rates will become higher, and it may require a little more for you to be approved. As your score decreases, you can see the trend. Lenders are less likely to give you optimal treatment. Lastly, those who fall in the 300-600 category are considered to have poor credit. You may only be approved for secured cards and secured loans with high interest rates, or possibly an unsecured credit limit of only $200-$500.

Your credit score matters; lenders will run your credit before financing your loan. However, other determining factors are considered when reviewing your credit report. It's important to maintain a good credit score, but that's not the only thing that is important. I quickly learned that there was more to credit than having a high score. If it were just a high score that was important, I would have gotten the job at the credit union. However, there are so many contributing factors that tell a complete story about each of us. Our credit report reveals how trustworthy we really are. It also tells a story about our foundation, stability, management skills, our present conditions and trustworthiness. Prior to not being hired at the credit union, I felt that I was very trustworthy and dependable. I never considered how my credit report could validate or invalidate specific characteristics about me. When you apply for a car loan, house loan, or credit cards, the first thing lenders want to know before they help is if you are trustworthy. They need to know not only that they will get their money back, but also if they will make money off you. Lenders need to know the likelihood that you will payback your debt on time, plus they want to ensure that they receive the interest that you owe. Have you ever applied for a loan and received it just because you "said" you were trustworthy and that you would pay it back before time? Absolutely not! The reason is that lenders are not taking your word for it. They first want to validate who your credit says you are. You can show up in your best outfit and have the most positive attitude, but it all boils down to your credit report.

Credit Bureaus

Credit applications are submitted to the Credit Bureaus: Equifax, Experian, and Transunion. Credit Bureaus are not the authors of our credit narratives. Their job is to provide information that lenders use to help them to make important lending decisions. When it comes to employment, credit bureaus provide information that employers need to make an important employment decision. I have been asked if all three bureaus contain the same information. The answer is that the information that each have is remarkably similar. They all have the same categories: identifying information, credit accounts, credit inquiries, and public records. However, there may be an account that is reporting to Transunion as paid on time that may be reporting to Equifax or Experian as a late payment. This can cause variations in the scores. Some lenders will use a 3-Bureaus Credit Report. The 3-Bureaus Credit Report shows all three of your reports and scores on one report. The greatest advice I can give to maintain good credit is to pay your bills before time. Keep in mind that paying your bills "on time" is essentially paying your bills "before time." I understand that there are periods in life where we face adversities, but I want to challenge you to continue writing your story. If your credit is great, continue writing a great story. If your credit is poor, start writing a better story. Again, let me remind you that the power to write your story is completely up to you. Do not get upset with the information that is in the credit bureaus' database. Instead of getting upset, use that energy to create better habits that will enhance your credit report. The information that your credit report provides will determine the level of access you have to the things you desire. If you do not like the story that is being told about you, then it is time that you began educating yourself on what you need to do to change it.

Inquiries

You can start changing the narrative of your story by working to change your present conditions. 10% of your credit score and report is allocated to your inquiries. FICO refers to this 10% as "new credit." There are two different types of inquiries: a hard inquiry and a soft inquiry. Let's first discuss a hard inquiry. When you authorize a lender to look at your credit report, it results in a hard inquiry. When you review your report, you will see that lender listed on your credit report. From my experience, a hard inquiry can drop your credit score anywhere from 2-11 points, depending on what is in your file. The higher your score, the more points you may lose from an inquiry. If you have a thin credit file, your credit score can take a bigger hit. Now that we understand that a hard inquiry has the potential to harm your score, let's discuss how a soft inquiry is different. A soft inquiry doesn't show up on your credit report or have the ability to drop your score. Also, you will not know when a soft credit check is done because it will not show up on your report. An example of a soft inquiry is when an employer screens your credit.

There is no way around credit inquiries when applying for new credit. If you apply for a loan in the same industry, it will typically be treated as a single inquiry. Lenders are more lenient when you are shopping for a home. Therefore, if you are in the market shopping for a home, you may go to more than one bank because you are shopping around for the best interest rate. The inquiry may be classified as one inquiry in a certain time span. Typically, this will be treated as one inquiry within 45 days. For loans that are commonly involved in rate shopping, those inquiries will not be classified as separate inquiries and they will not negatively impact your score.

The information obtained from your credit report will help lenders to better understand your present conditions. This will help to consider if you are a high risk or low risk. Studies show that if you have six or more inquiries in one year, you are more likely to file for bankruptcy. Your FICO score refers to your present conditions as new credit. Although FICO score only considers inquiries from the last 12 months as new credit, those inquiries remain on your credit report for 24 months. When lenders are viewing your credit report, they can determine if you are in a crisis, if your back is up against a wall, or if you are in desperate need of money based on your credit inquiries. Inquiries have a greater impact if you have a short credit history or if you have few accounts. Inquiries are a minor component of your credit report, only making up 10% of your FICO score. The most important factor is how you pay your bills. You may wonder how your credit report can provide information about your current conditions? Here is an example: If you get into a car accident and total out your car, you then enter the market to finance a new one. If you go to several dealerships looking for a new vehicle and you allow each dealership to run your credit, then those inquiries will show up on your credit report. Lenders can interpret your present condition as you really needing a vehicle. Those inquiries can make it appear that you are in desperate need of a vehicle.

Your present conditions allow lenders to see if a new account was recently opened.

As I began to understand that credit was more than a score, I started to better understand why I wasn't the ideal candidate on paper. Being a victim of identity theft caused me to have several inaccurate accounts. It appeared that I lacked discipline and delayed gratification. Patience is necessary when building good habits because it can decipher between you receiving approval for $500 or $25,000. Understanding that 10% of your credit report is made up of new credit, you should be more conscious when opening new accounts.

Credit Power Knowledge

1. Credit Categories & Scores
    a. Excellent 800-850
    b. Very Good 750-799
    c. Good 700-749
    d. Fair 650-699
    e. Poor 600-649
    f. Very Bad 300-599

2. Having a high credit score only tells a portion of the story regarding your credit history.
3. Your credit report is made up of 10% of your present conditions, which FICO refers to as "new credit."
4. There are two different types of inquiries: hard inquiry & soft inquiry.
    a. When you authorize a lender to look at your credit report, it results in a hard inquiry.

  b. A soft inquiry does not show up on your credit report; neither can it drop your score.

5. Your present conditions will tell if you are risky or if, in a crisis, you are likely to file for bankruptcy.

Empowerment through Education: Lesson 1

Now that you understand that your credit report reveals more than just your score, be sure that you consider the 10% that provides information about your current conditions when you are applying for new lines of credit. Use the following tips to help improve your credit report:

1. Be mindful of how often you apply for credit.
2. Do not apply for credit if it is not necessary. Applying for credit frequently can make you appear, that you're in a crisis situation.
3. A hard inquiry can drop your credit score anywhere from 2-11 points, depending on what is in your file.

4. Ask yourself if the line of credit that you are applying for makes you look risky or more stable.

2

Foundation

Have you ever driven past a construction site? There are specific factors that are taken into consideration before building. Naturally, when you think of a foundation, you think about a supporting structure. Just like before a home is built, the home's foundation must be sturdy and consist of the proper materials so that as the building process begins, everything stays intact. I use this analogy because FICO refers to this section as your credit mixture. Your credit mixture consists of revolving and installment credit, which I like to refer to as the foundation of your credit report. Although they are different, having both helps to strengthen your credit overall.

Installment Loans

Installment loans consist of a large lump sum of money. Your installment loans show your ability to pay back money you owe. Installment loans can consist of student loans, car loans, or mortgages, etc., and requires fixed payments on the loan until it is paid off. Once paid off, installment loans close. Installment loans show that you can make a set payment at a set time over a long period of time.

Revolving Credit

Revolving credit consists of credit cards, retail cards, gas cards, etc. As you pay revolving credit, you then have access to a renewed balance once it is paid off. A good credit mix can help you to increase your credit score if you properly manage your accounts. Revolving credit is different from installment loans. With installment loans, there is an end date; however, with revolving credit, there is no end date as long as you pay on the balance. Installments have set payment plans limiting the flexibility, while revolving credit is flexible with payments, allowing you to pay a minimum payment or more. Revolving is not a fixed amount like a loan; the amount on the revolving credit account can be reused.

Credit Mixture

Let's consider a flower. In order for the flower to reach its full potential, it needs both water and sunlight. It can grow a little with just water, but it will be weak and will eventually shrivel up because it gets its energy from sunlight. If you want your flower to grow to its full potential, you create an environment with both water and sunlight. I used this analogy to help you understand why it's important to have a good credit mix. Having just installment loans will help to establish your credit, but it may be weak credit. However, adding in revolving credit will help to both strengthen and improve your credit. Revolving credit has a greater impact on your credit report than installment loans. Revolving credit holds more weight. Although you may have a $30,000 car loan and a $1,000 credit card limit, the credit card's impact is greater because it tells a story about the way you manage your money, and it is a part of the second largest component of your credit report. Remember we talked about present conditions in the previous chapter? Your present conditions and the foundation of your credit works together. Your credit card utilization contributes to the story that credit bureaus provide to the lenders about you. The way you handle your credit card is a reflection of the way you handle your finances. Remember, your credit report not only tells a story about your credit, but it also tells a story about what your character looks like on paper. Do you pay your bills on time? Do you overspend? Both things can be answered by reviewing your credit report. As we continue to explore the information conveyed in your credit report, you will begin to clearly see how your credit report creates a narrative about your behavior and your character.

The foundation of your credit report tells if you are able to multitask. How so? Can you pay your installment loans and your credit card bills at the same time, on time? Paying both revolving credit and installments shows your flexibility with paying a set amount each month, as well as a fluctuating amount each month. Putting your needs over your wants is one of the significant factors that helps individuals build and maintain good credit. As I shared with you previously, maintaining good credit can inhibit you from being selected from specific career advancements. When employers are reviewing your credit report, they are looking for character clues. They want to know if you are flexible, versatile, or if you can multitask. It is important because employers want to maximize your skillset in various positions. Employers are paying you for being an asset, not a liability. If you are not able to perform multiple tasks well simultaneously, then employers do not feel that they are getting what they are paying you for. Reviewing your credit report helps employers in the selection process of hiring new candidates. We often attribute credit only to purchases, but I want you to broaden your perspective on how your credit can impact your life in more than one way.

Now that you better understand that credit mix makes up 10% of your credit score, maintaining installment and revolving accounts are essential components necessary to receive the maximum credit score. Your credit score is calculated from a mathematical algorithm. The information in your report is what creates your 3-digit score. The credit score algorithm yields the maximum score when both types of credit accounts are present on your credit report.

Credit Repair

For those of you working to repair your credit, there are necessary steps you need to take. First, you need to order a copy of your credit report. This will help you to gain a better understanding of how creditors and lenders view your character on paper. You can get your free credit report once a year from www.annualreport.com. If you need help reading your credit report, you can schedule a free consultation at www.creditpowerllc.com or you can call 888-937-3379.

When you review your report, look for inaccuracies. This provides you with the information needed to dispute items on your credit. Items on your credit report that you don't recognize can be a sign of fraudulent activity. Make sure you know the difference between things that may not be yours and things that may be inaccurate. *Credit Power, LLC* can assist you with re-establishing credit and creating the foundation needed to improve your credit score.

As you work to repair your credit, you should begin seeing an increase in your score. It is your responsibility to develop good habits to continue building your credit, meaning you have an obligation to pay back what you owe and make payments on time. Even the bible speaks of good stewardship and how important it is to be trustworthy in everything that we do, *"Moreover it is required in stewardship, that a man be found faithful" – 1 Corinthians 4:2.* I understand that there are unfortunate circumstances that may arise that may get you off track; however, I challenge you to continue working to build good credit. As you develop the consistent routine of paying your bills on time, this will reflect in your credit report, and you will gain access to more of the things you desire. Not paying your bills makes you a liability, and it makes it more difficult for you to gain access to the things you need and desire.

One of the most valuable lessons that I have learned from re-establishing the foundation of my credit is that until I established a good credit mix, I limited myself to what I could have. By building a solid credit foundation, I can live without limits and build generational wealth. I am proud that over the years, I have been able to help hundreds of individuals re-establish the foundation of their credit. Through my company, *Credit Power, LLC*, I have been able to help various individuals from high school students to those with a PHD. You may be wondering why someone who is established and has a PHD need assistance with credit. It is because your income is not calculated in your 3-digit credit score; in fact, your income is nowhere on your credit report. Therefore, it does not matter how much money you earn. Many believe that it is impossible to re-establish their credit, and the thought of what it requires is daunting before they have the knowledge. However, as they learn more of what it requires to establish and rebuild credit, they are then equipped with the tools to change their lives. I am an example that it is possible. It's easy to believe that you can't have better if you are not educated on how to receive better. You are now taking your power back as you empower yourself through education. As you gain more knowledge, it is up to you to apply the knowledge you have received and create change. Everything worth building should always first start with a solid foundation.

Credit Power Knowledge

1. The foundation of your credit makes up 10% of your credit report. FICO refers to this section as "Credit Mixture."
2. Credit mixture consists of both installment loans & revolving credit.
3. Lenders determine if you are a good candidate for approval based off of the way you borrow and payback.
4. Revolving and installment accounts are the foundation of a credit report. However, revolving credit is highly important in the calculation of credit utilization, which is the second largest component (after credit history) that makes up your credit score.

5. Employers and lenders determine if you are able to multitask or if you are flexible based on the foundation portion of your credit report.

Empowerment through Education: Lesson 2

Now that you have been educated on the foundation portion of your credit report, you are now empowered to use the following tips to help improve your credit report.

1. Order a copy of your credit report from www.annualreport.com.
2. Review your credit report and determine if you have both installment loans and revolving credit (credit card).
3. If you need help reading your credit report, you can schedule a free consultation at www.creditpowerllc.com or you can call 888-937-3379.

4. Be sure to make all of your payments on time. Remember that on time means before time.
5. Keep your credit card balance below 7% especially 1 week before the statement closing date. Your SCD (statement closing date) is normally a few days after the due date. Call your credit card company to determine the exact date.

3

Stability

There was once a time in my life when I wanted nothing more than stability. During that time, I wasn't at all concerned with financial freedom or creating generational wealth. I just wanted to create a stable life for my daughter and myself. Temporary jobs and struggling to make ends meet became exhausting. My mental health was suffering, as stress and depression seemed to be taking over my life. I was living day-to-day without a solid plan. My lack of stability was affecting every area of my life. It was even affecting my credit score. At the time, I thought I was doing a good job covering up the adversities I was facing.

I did not know that my private struggles would make a public appearance on my credit report one day. Credit stability, which FICO refers to as "length of credit history," makes up 15% of your calculated credit score. My lack of stability was apparent in my credit report. I was doing everything in my power to survive. My credit report revealed that I was living in a crisis. Survival mode was hectic for me. I had no peace, and I was always racking my brain worrying how things would work out. I felt like nothing was in my control. Not getting the job at the credit union opened my eyes to learn so much about my credit and myself. My credit report showed that I did a poor job keeping commitments and I wasn't very reliable. Being a victim of identity theft and fraud revealed character flaws of others who had taken advantage of me. It was not my character that was being displayed in my credit report. I never thought of myself as being unreliable. After an in-depth review of my credit report, I realized that my credit report was painting a negative picture of who I was. My character on paper didn't match the way I described myself to others. My credit was so messed up from being a victim of identity theft. The work that I did to maintain a good score was overshadowed by those who were mismanaging accounts in my name. It became clearer to me why I was not viewed as the ideal candidate for the position. What employer wants to hire someone who doesn't come across as trustworthy on paper? I refused to allow my character to reflect the behaviors of others. As I began to review my credit, I found out that it wasn't a stranger that had stolen my identity. It was actually my family members. Those family members had, at some point in my life, helped take care of me, so I felt like I owed it to them to let it go. I came from an environment where we weren't taught that the things we do in our everyday life have the ability to affect our credit. Although I had been done wrong by some of my close family members, I did not have the time to spend all of my energy blaming them. It was completely up to me to work to re-establish my credit. I didn't know where to begin. I can recall feeling defeated before I even started working on the credit repair process. However, I was not willing to allow my credit report to tell a false story about my character. I work with several clients who have significant challenges with their credit. After we work together and they see their lives changing, it makes everything that I have been through seem worth it. I sometimes think to myself what my life would be like if I had given up after not getting the job at the credit union or if I had let it define me. What if I had allowed my narrative to stay the same? Truth is, I would still be in financial captivity. I openly share my truth about my life because I need others to see me and see possibility. I want you to know that you are your only limit. Therefore, if you are not changing your life that means there is something within you that is holding you back. Sometimes the changes that we make seem too small and insignificant, but remember that a thousand miles begins with one step.

Re-establishing Relationships

After months of being in a deep depression, I pulled myself together and began working towards changing my life for the better. I started cleaning up my credit and establishing better relationships with lenders and bill collectors. I began to understand the significance of stability when I started working on my credit. Being stable is more than just having a good job. Sure, having a good job is helpful due to the steady income; however, your behavior must also change to manage your funds to create and maintain stability. Your credit is a reflection of your behavior. How you handle your bills will also shine a light on how you will manage your job, your relationships, and so much more.

Length of credit history shows the amount of time you are in relationship with a lender or creditor. Typically, the longer the credit history, the more positive the impact it will have on your score. Therefore, be sure that you are not closing those old accounts. Closing an account can have a negative impact on your credit score due to the reduction in age. I am not referring to your actual age, but the average age of your accounts on your credit report, especially if that account has been open for several years. The reason is because the age of your account is calculated into your 3-digit credit score. The longer your accounts are open, the more trustworthy you appear to lenders. A long-term relationship history with lenders provides you with a greater likelihood of credit approval. The perks of having a long-term relationship means lower interest rates and it also saves you money, which can be used towards other things. Use caution when making decisions regarding closing your accounts. For example, when you apply for a home loan, lenders pay very close attention to your actions. Therefore, closing out an account can reduce your score and make you appear as unstable.

Having older accounts in good standing is better than having a new account. A proven track record of great behavior can be validated through long-term account history. According to FICO, a longer credit history always impacts your credit score in a positive way. Therefore, when you are first establishing credit, it is common that you will have to allow time for your accounts to age.

Authorized User

In the event that you don't have time to establish credit and you are trying to qualify for a home or a vehicle quickly, you can be added as an authorized user to a responsible family member's or friend's credit card account with age. The age from their accounts will be transferred to your credit report, giving you backdated history. A common industry name for "authorized user" is also known as a tradeline. The tradeline can be either a revolving or an installment credit account. The information that is included in the tradeline is calculated into your 3-digit credit score; it's not the tradeline itself. Before my daughter turned 18, I did this for her. I added her to three of my credit cards, and this boosted her to a score of 767. That is what I gave my daughter for her 18th birthday. I literally allowed her to piggyback off my credit, which gave her a head start in life.

For those of you who are just starting to build your credit history, you may be denied when applying for new credit. It is not because your credit is bad, but because you do not have enough credit history. Think about it: Would you allow a barber who just graduated cosmetology school to cut your hair for your prom or your wedding? No, because they haven't cut hair long enough to make you feel comfortable with them not making a mistake. The less experience they have, the greater the chances are that they may mess up your hair. The less experience they have, the greater risk they are. Creditors and lenders feel the same way about approving you for new credit with high limits if you do not have validating experience. You would not give a seven-year-old $20 and tell them to go into the candy store but not spend it all, right? They would spend it all at once because they do not have experience with managing that amount of money. Now you understand why it can be difficult to build credit when you are new to credit. Before the age of 18, most young adults are considered ghosts, because no one can see them on paper. This shouldn't be a deterrent from working towards building credit. There are solutions to help resolve the issue of not having a credit history. As we previously discussed, you can be added as an authorized user to someone's existing account, or you can work to establish your credit using a secured credit card or a secured loan.

If you do not have any bankruptcies, you can instantly be approved for a secured credit card or a secured loan. You can visit www.creditpowerllc.com and click on the tab that says, "financial products" and apply. A secured credit card is where you pay cash upfront to receive a line of credit. Essentially, you are creating your credit limit by presenting the funds up front. The secured credit card or secured loan will help you build credit the same way you would if you were approved for a traditional credit card or installment loan. I recommend you use your secured card for the bills you currently pay. For example, if you pay a monthly cell phone bill or purchase groceries, instead of using your debit card or cash, you can use your secured credit card. This way, you gain points that will raise your credit score by doing what you are already accustomed to doing. *Credit Power* also offers a financial product called a CD (certificate of deposit), that reports to all three credit bureaus. Keep in mind, CD's are offered by banking institutions, but theirs do not report to all three credit bureaus.

As you work diligently to take care of your credit, you will build up your length of credit history to positively impact 15% of your overall credit report. In the previous chapter, we discussed how lenders view your foundation (revolving & installment credit) to determine risk. By now, my prayer is that you are beginning to see how each component of your credit history works together to create a narrative about your character, habits, and behavior. If you aren't happy with the narrative, then you must do the work to change it. You must practice establishing a good relationship with your lenders and creating stability within your life. When you sign your name on the dotted line, you are committing to taking care of your responsibilities. No matter how small the credit line is or how insignificant the bill may be, it would be best if you always took care of your credit, so that credit can take care of you. The more reliable you are, the more access you will have to the things that you desire. Scripture speaks of faithfulness and being a good steward over what is given to you, *"One who is faithful in very little is also faithful in much, and one who is dishonest in very little is also dishonest in much." – Luke 16:10.*

Instability creates additional life stressors. I know firsthand about enduring stressful situations. The stress, depression, and anxiety that I suffered was challenging to overcome. Research studies suggest that there is a link between poor credit and mental health. The continuous stress of debt and other financial obligations leaves individuals suffering from both depression and anxiety. Fighting through mental health issues while also working to overcome economic disparities can be challenging. I had to fight through depression to create a better life for my child and myself. I worked diligently to create stability by staying in long and healthy relationships with creditors, lenders, and employers. It didn't happen overnight; it took time. Once I became stable, it gave me access to more. It has allowed me to create generational wealth for my child and my grandchild. But I first had to get myself together, making sure I had above an 830 credit score. (FICO score ranges from 300-850). The only way I felt comfortable adding my daughter as an authorized user to my existing credit cards was by first making sure I was stable. If my accounts were not in good standing, she would have adopted bad credit. By me taking excellent care of my credit, it took care of me and my daughter, and now my two-year-old grandson. I recently bought my grandson his second home -- five bedrooms, three bathrooms, and a two-car-garage. This is the definition of true generational wealth. I am sharing my truth because I want every reader to know that you have the power to change your life despite your circumstances. Nothing is impossible; everything we do begins with a thought. If you can think about it, you can obtain it, but you must be willing to do the work it requires: *"Lazy hands make for poverty, but diligent hands bring wealth" –Proverbs 10:4.*

Perhaps you're like me; I didn't grow up in a stable environment. On September 12, 1984, when I was 6 years old, my mother was killed. I will never forget that day because I was in the house when it happened. I remember sitting on my mother's lap as her boyfriend was telling her that he was going to leave and crash his car. He was upset about something that happened with him and his brother. She tried her best to calm him down, but he was outraged. She pleaded with him not to leave, but she couldn't stop him. My last memory of my mother being alive is her telling me to go and lock the doors and go to bed. That night when I went to bed, I did not know that would be the last time seeing my mother alive. That night, I was awakened by banging and screams of, "She's dead! She's dead!" I looked over the balcony and I saw my mother laying in a puddle of smeared blood. One of her eyes was removed from the socket, and she laid there breathless. My mother was gone, and my siblings and I were left with nothing. My mother did not have an insurance policy. She wasn't stable throughout her life, so I didn't know what stability was. After my mother passed away, I went to live with my father. That was short lived because my father was abusive. I then went to live with my sister until I was 16; she took care of me during that time. After that, I went to live in my other sister's home for about two years until I went to Job Corps, and then to the military. On September 12, 2004, exactly 20 years to the date that my mother was killed, my father died. Here I was, a young mother, left in the world with no parents, trying my best to be a good parent to my daughter. The first time I ever truly experienced stability was in 2006 when I finally moved away from my hometown of Pittsburgh to Virginia. I finally created a home for my daughter and me. I've had to work extremely hard throughout my life.

Through my unfortunate experience with losing my mother when I was a young child, I have vowed to create a much better life for my daughter. When the day comes, and the Good Lord calls me home, she will not be left with nothing, which is the way my mother left my siblings and me. We had absolutely nothing left for us to inherit. I have worked hard to put things in place to be sure that she has a great inheritance, and that my grandchildren and their children remember my name. She will be able to continue living a stable life and continue building generational wealth.

Credit Power Knowledge

1. The length of credit history (stability) makes up 15% of your credit report.
2. Credit stability helps lenders determine risk of the borrower.
3. The length of credit history helps to determine your reliability.
4. Secure credit cards and secure loans can help to build your length of credit history.
5. A common industry name for "authorized user" is also known as a tradeline. The tradeline can be either a revolving or an installment credit account.

Empowerment through Education: Lesson 3

Now that you have been educated on how creating a stable credit history makes up 15% of your FICO score, you are now empowered to use the following tips to help improve your overall credit report.

1. It is not too late to work towards repairing your credit.
2. Improving your credit history will help you to improve your life.
3. Creating stability is necessary for creating generational wealth.
4. Get a secured credit card or secured loan and keep the balance low.

5. You can visit www.creditpowerllc.com and apply for a secured card by clicking on the tab that says, "financial products" and apply.
6. In the event that you don't have time to establish credit and you are trying to qualify for a home or a vehicle quickly, you can be added to a responsible family member's or friend's credit card account with age, as an authorized user.

4

Management Skills

By now, you understand that your credit report tells a story about you and how you manage your life, finances and, in some instances, your relationships. Understanding your credit report fundamentals gives you all the tools you need to manage your credit properly. Previously, we discussed new credit, credit mix, and length of credit history. Together, those components make up 35% of your calculated credit score. However, the management skill component of your credit report, which FICO refers to as "amounts owed," makes up 30% of your credit score. This is the portion where creditors and lenders determine how you manage your money, by the credit utilization of your credit card. Amounts owed is the second largest component of your credit score. Naturally, when you think about the amounts owed, you think of how much debt you have. How many accounts do you have open that you still owe money on? When you are close to maxing out your credit card, balance creditors and lenders perceive this as you not being able to properly manage your debt. According to FICO, the behavior patterns of individuals with high scores show that they consistently make payments on time, revolving balances are kept low, and they only apply for credit when they need it.

Credit Utilization

The amounts owed on your report focuses on how you manage your debt. I strongly recommend you always consider your credit utilization. Credit utilization is your balance in comparison to your available credit limit. For example, if you have a credit card with a $500 limit and your balance is $35, then you are at 7% credit utilization. Another example is if you have a credit card with a $500 limit and the balance on this card is $400, you are at 80% of your credit utilization, which makes you appear to be a higher risk. If you are constantly maxing out credit cards, this can cause you to be viewed as a liability to lenders. Remember, the lower your balance before the statement closes, the more points you will gain to raise your score. I recommend your credit card balance be no more than 7% when the statement closes. The statement closing date is when your balance will be reported to the credit bureau. When creditors and lenders review this portion of your credit report, they are looking to see how much debt you have, how you manage your accounts, if you are living above your means, and if you can afford what you are applying for. Lenders are looking to see how well you manage your debt overall and how your credit is being used. The greater of a risk you appear to be, the higher your interest rates will be and the more money you will spend. Remember, your credit determines your level of accessibility to the things that you need and desire.

As we drill further down into your credit report's management skills, I want you to consider what your credit report says about you. While you are reading this portion of the book, I want to challenge you to take self-inventory of the way you manage your accounts. We often hear people only refer to their credit score, but you have now been educated that lenders are looking at more than just your score before approving you for credit. The management skills portion of your credit report shows how much credit experience you have. If you do not have a credit card, it looks as if you don't have any experience with credit. The more experience you have, the higher limits of credit you will be approved for. What does your credit utilization say about you? It shows if you know how to manage your money, if you are patient, or if you are experiencing a financial crisis. Your credit utilization on your revolving credit measures how much available credit you have. If you are maxing out your credit cards and paying the bill on time, but making the minimum payment, this still shows you may struggle with financial discipline. Your spending habits are reflected in this section of your report. Low utilization of your credit limit can have a positive impact on your overall credit score. Do you live above your means? Are you trying to keep up with those around you? Are material possessions pushing you further away from obtaining financial freedom? Are you working towards building generational wealth? In the world that we live in today, it's so easy to get caught up in driving fancy cars, owning the biggest home, or wearing all of the designer clothing. Let me be clear, there is absolutely nothing wrong with having nice things. We all deserve to enjoy the luxuries of life, but we must be wise in the way we obtain those luxuries. Social media makes it easy to see the way people live, and it appears that everyone is thriving. However, the truth of the matter is we do not have access to everyone's credit report or their bank accounts through a social media post. You may be trying to keep up with someone who is struggling to keep up with his or her own lifestyle. It is important that you do not become overly consumed with what appears to be success from the outside. The reality is, we are all struggling in some area of our lives that others may perceive or interpret as success. It is imperative that you maintain a lifestyle that fits your financial environment. For example, someone who earns a million dollars, but also spends a million dollars is broke. However, someone who earns $50,000 but only spends $20,000 is managing their money better. It is not about how much money you make; rather, it is more about how you manage your money and how well you make your money work for you. Many of the people we admire who are living lavishly are also living lavishly above their means. For example, someone may dress up in the finest designer clothes, but they could be dressing up the part of them that doesn't feel worthy. Do not try to make your income fit someone else's lifestyle. This is why it's so important not to compare your life to others. You must run your own race at your own pace. You can have all the things you desire, but first educate yourself on building and reestablishing your credit before you create a lifestyle that is hard to maintain with bad debt. You have the power to change the narrative of your life. Living above your means leads to more issues that will inevitably impact your credit negatively. Statistically, those who live above their means are more likely to have a poor credit score. When your credit is poor, it makes it more difficult to obtain the things you desire. Do you really want to drive a luxury car with a 24% interest rate, which will cause you to pay far more for the car than it is worth? Or would you like to drive that same luxury car with a 3% interest rate, saving you thousands of dollars? I am not telling you that you shouldn't pursue the things you desire, but I'm encouraging you to do it the right way. Do not overextend yourself by maxing out your credit cards, owing tons of money to multiple lines of credit, or by maxing out your available credit limit. Today, I am able to drive the vehicles of my dreams, live in a beautiful home, own multiple properties, and create generational wealth. Building good credit put me in the position to have the things I desire and the ability to take care of my family. Maintaining a high credit score and healthy credit report put me in a position to be approved for high credit limits. It took me years before I was invited to receive a black card. Most people only hear about black cards in music videos or reality shows for the rich and famous. I am here to let you know that it is possible for you, as well. I had to learn to be okay with delayed gratification. It was imperative that I became educated on how to build and maintain good credit. Without going through the pain and hardships of being taken advantage of and without the knowledge I have today, I wouldn't be in this position. Putting off the things that I wanted back then has given me access to far more today. It is not just about having good credit that's important; managing your credit is also very important.

Credit Power Knowledge

1. The amounts owed makes up 30% of your credit score.
2. Your credit utilization affects your overall credit score.
3. Statistically, those who live above their means are more likely to have a poor credit score.
4. The amounts owed on your credit report reflects your credit experience, responsibilities, and spending habits.
5. The greater of a risk you appear to be, the higher your interest rates will be.

6. Lenders are looking to see how well you manage your debt overall and how your credit is being used.

Empowerment through Education: Lesson 4

Now that you have learned that the amount of debt you owe makes up 30% of your FICO score, you are now empowered to use the following tips to help improve your overall credit report.

1. Always consider how much of your available credit is currently occupied before applying for new credit.
2. Maxing out your credit card can lower your score even if you pay your credit card bill on time.

3. Your credit card balance should be no more than 7% when the statement closes.
4. Living above your means increases the likelihood of your credit score dropping.
5. Practice discipline when it comes to spending. Delayed gratification is still gratification.

5

Trustworthy

"Give to everyone what you owe them: If you owe taxes, pay taxes; if revenue, then revenue; if respect, then respect; if honor, then honor" –Romans 13:7.

The final component of your credit report we will discuss is your payment history. Your payment history makes up 35% of your credit report. This section makes up the largest percentage of your overall credit score. Lenders want to know the same thing, and that is if they can trust you to pay what you owe and if they can make money off the money that they allowed you to borrow. No one likes to loan money to someone who is not going to pay it back. Have you ever loaned someone money and they promised that they would pay you back by a specific date, but didn't? If they fail to pay you back, then you are less likely to allow them to borrow money in the future. However, if they make good on their word and they ever need to borrow money again, you are more likely to do so without hesitation. Loaning money to someone who isn't trustworthy decreases your chances of ever being repaid. Would you knowingly lend money to someone who had a bad track record of repayment? Probably not! Lenders check in with credit bureaus to review your payment history before agreeing to an approval. If your credit report tells the story that you are a thief and a liar, lenders will not lend you money. How can your credit report determine if you are a thief or liar? Great question! If you have a collection/charge-off on your credit report that may indicate that you did not pay what you owed for at least six months straight. Due to your lack of payment, lenders can access your character on paper. Your payment history reveals if you have paid your bills on time, if you've paid them in full, or if you have skipped payments. Essentially, your payment history answers the number one question -- are you trustworthy? When I applied for the credit union job, the company did not hire me because of the collections/charge-offs on my report. My character on paper did not display that I was trustworthy due to the delinquent accounts on my report. To them, it looked like I didn't keep my word when it came to satisfying my financial obligations. They may have wondered how I could properly manage others' accounts when I was poorly managing my own accounts? At the time, I was not aware of the fraudulent activities on my credit report. Unfortunately, I came across as a liar and as if I wasn't trustworthy. I kept watch at my credit score, but I did not review each component of my credit report. Understanding your credit report is important because it tells a story about you. It is completely up to you to make sure the information that is reported is accurate and reflects your character in a positive light. This information is not only for creditors and lenders, but also for landlords, insurance companies, and employers.

Late Payments

Can late payments destroy your score? Payments that are 30 or more days past due have the potential to drop your score over 100 points. Therefore, your credit can take a major hit if you have a negative payment history. By federal law, a late payment cannot be reported to the credit bureaus before it is 30 days past due. Keep in mind that although it may not be reported to the credit bureaus, it may result in interest and late fee. If you're on a tight budget, interest and late fees can cause more issues with managing your finances. Therefore, I recommend paying your bills at least one week prior to the due date to save money on interest. Partial payments do not keep you from being reported to credit bureaus; however, setting up a payment arrangement that allows you to split the full payment before its due date may prevent a late payment from showing up on your credit report. When you formulate a contract between you and the lender, you agree to the terms and conditions of the contract. Failure to keep your end of the agreement will have a negative impact on your credit report. If you have gone past the 30-day mark, you need to bring your account current. The longer you allow the account to go without payment, the more damage you do to your credit. Also, keep in mind that your score is made up of more than just one component, as we discussed. It is not just about paying something on your bills; paying your bills on time for the full obligated amount is just as important. Delinquent accounts can cause great harm to your overall credit score. The amount of money you owe on an account can also weigh heavily on your payment history. We discussed previously how revolving credit could be more impactful than installment loans. Therefore, delinquent and overdue payments on your credit cards are extremely harmful to your credit score. The longer you allow your account to remain in a delinquent status, the more you run the risk of your account going into collections. Once this happens, the status of the account can never be changed back to positive. Even paying the balance in full will not allow the status of the account to have a positive reputation on your report. You will need to have the entire account removed as if it were never there. If not, the status of the account will always say collection/charge-off. A collection/charge-off on your report is an indication that creditors and lenders no longer expect to receive payments from you. When this happens, the next step is usually for the original creditor to send the account to a third-party collection agency. The collection agency is added to your credit report and shows up as a new derogatory item on your report. This happens because items that are charged-off still count as outstanding debt that must be paid. You can work with credit repair companies, such as my company, *Credit Power, LLC*, to have accounts deleted for its inaccuracies. You may also work with the collection agencies to either pay the full amount of your debt, or you can settle with them and make a partial payment if the account is accurate. Keep in mind; settling the debt will not change the status from collection/charge-off. However, if you are trying to get approved for a mortgage, the lender may recommend you settle your account before receiving an approval. Ultimately, you should avoid having an unpaid or unsettled account on your credit report. I suggest that you set your bills up with auto-draft; this will allow payments to come out of your account automatically, if you have the funds in your account.

Budgeting is a useful tip to help you to make payments on time. You need to know how much money you earn, how much money you can afford to spend each month, and how much money you need to save. To budget successfully, you have to know exactly how much money you have coming in weekly, bi-monthly, monthly, or quarterly. Once you have this information, you subtract all the expenses. Your budget should include a savings. If you have a savings, you can have funds for unexpected situations that may arise. If you do not have a savings, you run the risk of dismantling your budget, and this could cause a downward spiral to your endeavors to build and maintain good credit. Your savings account is just as important as your expense account. The money left over is the money that can be used to level up. Leveling up is simply going to the next level. Challenging yourself to better, smarter and more productive overall. I challenge you to level up in your finances, level up in the way you pay your bills, level up so that you can enjoy financial freedom.

Having good credit is the key to financial freedom, building wealth and creating generational wealth.

Financial Freedom

To me, financial freedom is having enough residual income to take care of your living expenses. The number one way to acquire financial freedom is by educating yourself on money and generating passive income. Passive income is money you earn that requires minimum effort to maintain. Even if you work a job, you still need passive income to help you to establish financial freedom. You don't have to be rich to obtain financial freedom. However, having financial freedom is having enough to cover your expenses so that you can spend your time doing what you love and less time working. Once you have financial freedom, you are no longer living paycheck to paycheck. You remove the chains that bind you to a 9-5 and working becomes an option, not an obligation. Financial freedom, for me, is being able to abruptly take a mental health day without worrying about being paid for FMLA. I have the flexibility to prioritize my health and my family over my job. Overall, financial freedom allows you to enjoy life without going broke while doing so and provides you with the foundation to build wealth.

Wealth

I define wealth as income-producing assets that produce passive income. Examples of passive income include; rental properties, vending machines, selling an eBook online, investing in the stock market. Your passive income may require an upfront investment, but eventually these streams of income will grow, and generate consistent revenue without much labor on your part. When you can go for long periods of time, without working while still paying all your bills and living the life you want to live, you will begin experiencing the benefits of your passive income. If you are anxious and stressing about where the money is coming from to cover your necessities, then you haven't built wealth. Making money in your sleep is a sign that you are building wealth. Waking up in the morning and seeing financial reports indicating successful transactions is a sign that you are on the path to building wealth. Essentially, building wealth requires that you have multiple streams of passive income. To determine if you are on the path to building wealth, start by calculating your passive income and determining how long your money will keep you afloat. Building wealth for yourself puts you in the position to also build generational wealth.

Generational Wealth

Generational wealth is assets that are passed down from one generation to the next. Stock, real estate, or a business are just some of the ways that you can pass down generational wealth. Creating wealth for yourself establishes the foundation for creating generational wealth. Your assets should outlive you and should be passed down to the next generation. Previously, I shared that I bought my grandson his second home. That is my way of building generational wealth through real estate. Having good credit opened the door for me to do so.

It's not too late to improve your credit and develop a good payment history. As you begin paying bills on time, you can work to get current on your bills and stay current. Older credit problems weigh less on your credit score. If you can become consistent with paying your bills on time, even after having significant problems in the past, you can still increase your credit score. There is no such thing as a permanent narrative unless you stop writing. You can continue writing your story by working actively towards positive change.

Credit Power Knowledge

1. Your payment history makes up 35% of your credit report.
2. Lenders check with credit bureaus to review your payment history before agreeing to an approval.
3. Your payment history provides lenders with the information needed to determine the likelihood that you will pay your debt.
4. Payments that are 30 or more days past due have the potential to drop your score over 100 points.
5. By federal law, a late payment cannot be reported to the credit bureaus before it is 30 days past due.
6. Bankruptcies will stay on your credit report for 7-10 years

7. Settling the debt will not change the status from collection/charge-off.
8. Passive income is money you earn that requires minimum effort to maintain.
9. Building wealth requires that you have multiple streams of passive income.

Empowerment through Education: Lesson 5

Now that you have been educated on the importance of keeping a good payment routine, you are now empowered to use the following tips to help improve your overall credit report.

1. Pay your bills at least one week prior to the due date to save money on interest.
2. Become consistent with paying your bills on time.
3. Create a budget for yourself.
4. Creating a budget helps you to pay bills on time.
5. Set your bills up with auto draft.
6. Work with *Credit Power, LLC* to help you rebuild your credit.

7. Calculate your passive income and determine how long your money will keep you afloat.

Conclusion

"Rise up; this matter is in your hands. We will support you, so take courage and do it." –Ezra 10:4

I started out with nothing, but today I am blessed beyond measure. Whatever your story currently is does not have to be the way your story ends. My disadvantage put me in a position to help thousands of people. I needed every part of my story to bring me to the place I am today. I am encouraged by the scripture, *"And we know that all things work together for good to them that love God, who are called according to his purpose" - Romans 8:28*. I do not make excuses about my past; I use everything that I have been through as fuel and ammunition to continue moving forward.

There are so many people out there who feel like I once did, but when I share my story, I open them up to a new world of possibilities. It does not matter where you are on your journey, you can improve, and you will. You will rebuild and create a brighter future. I get joy when I receive messages from clients sharing with me that their score has raised as little as 3 points. The joy they have about improving their score transfers over to me. Knowing that I am really helping to change people's life means the world to me. I help families move from a bad neighborhood to good neighborhoods. I help families living in rodent infested homes move into brand new homes. I empower parents to provide a better life for their families. By helping parents to get their credit together, their children benefit because they have the opportunity to grow up in better neighborhoods. They also have the opportunity to receive a better education. These significant changes open up our children to completely different life experiences. This gives them a fair chance at becoming major contributors in our society. I help women in abusive relationships, who feel stuck because of bad credit, free themselves and create a better life. They all begin opening themselves up to a new reality and so many more possibilities.

You, too, have the power to create stability in your life. Becoming stable may take time, but I can assure you that it is absolutely worth it. *"The race is not given to the swift, nor to the battle to the strong – (Ecclesiastes 9:11) but he who endures to the end" (Matthew 24:13).* If you are looking to repair or build your credit, it is not too late to start.

Many of us feel defeated before we ever get started. We quickly grow frustrated with the process when we do not see the value in it, and we give up easily when we don't have a paradigm for how to do it. When we do not have a representation of success around us, it can feel like our dreams are too big. Through my journey and my truth, I hope you will learn that rejection is just preparation for a bigger and better *yes*. Every time that you are told *no*, let it motivate you to go harder and put in more work. For me, *no* means "not yet." No means go back and get more prepared. No means you have more work to do. No means your time is right around the corner. No is not final unless I stop working towards it. Don't give up on your dreams, no matter the space that you are in today. You have been empowered through the information you have gathered from reading this book. You now have the knowledge to execute and change your life.

You have been running, ducking, and dodging long enough. It's time that you stop and confront your credit head on. You can't hide from bad credit. The sooner you address it, the sooner you will enjoy a better future. As you uncover the issues that led you down the path of financial captivity and poor credit, you empower yourself to make positive changes. Bad relationships with lenders may have started with one late payment, but you can develop new and thriving relationships by making a commitment that all your payments will be made on time from this point forward. Behavior is the driving force behind success of any magnitude. Whatever we consistently do will yield an outcome that is predicated upon our behavior. As you work towards changing your behavior, you will experience an improvement in your credit score that will lead you closer to financial freedom and on the path to creating generational wealth.

Understanding the power of credit and how it works is a unifying force that can improve the lives of individuals, families, and communities beyond the limitations of the status quo. You do not have to yield to false narratives. You have the power to write your story. Breaking the generational cycles of bad credit and financial captivity will start with you. You don't have to wait any longer. The rest of your life starts with this present moment.

There 's no other way but UP from here!

Made in the USA
Monee, IL
08 November 2026

67969856R00059